HAMILTON BEACH
BREAD MACHINE
COOKBOOK FOR BEGINNERS

The Best, Easy, Gluten-Free and

Foolproof recipes for your

Hamilton Beach Bread Machine

AMANDA COOK

Copyright

No part of this publication may be reproduced, stored in a retrieval system or transmitted in any form or by any means, electronic, mechanical, photocopying, recording, scanning or otherwise, except as permitted under Sections 107 or 108 of the 1976 United States Copyright Act, without the prior written permission of the Publisher. Requests to the Publisher for permission should be addressed to the Permissions Department.

Limit of Liability/Disclaimer of Warranty: The Publisher and the author make no representations or warranties with respect to the accuracy or completeness of the contents of this work and specifically disclaim all warranties, including without limitation warranties of fitness for a particular purpose. No warranty may be created or extended by sales or promotional materials. The advice and strategies contained herein may not be suitable for every situation. This work is sold with the understanding that the publisher is not engaged in rendering medical, legal or other professional advice or services.

If professional assistance is required, the services of a competent professional person should be sought. Neither the Publisher nor the author shall be liable for damages arising here from. The fact that an individual, organization or website is referred to in this work as a citation and/or potential source of further information does not mean that the author or the Publisher endorses the information the individual, organization or website may provide or recommendations they/it may make. Further, readers should be aware that Internet websites listed in this work might have changed or disappeared between when this work was written and when it is read.
The author publishes its books in a variety of electronic and print formats. Some content that appears in print may not be available in electronic books, and vice versa.

TRADEMARKS: All other trademarks are the property of their respective owners. The author is not associated with any product or vendor mentioned in this book

Table of Contents

Table of Contents   3

INTRODUCTION   7

Basic Bread   9

   Regular Soft White Loaf   9
   Healthy Bran Bread   10
   Pumpernickel Bread Loaf   11
   Soft Rye Bread   12
   Soft Egg Bread   13
   Golden Raisin Bread   14
   Whole Wheat Soda Bread   15
   Golden Corn Bread   16
   Peasant Bread   17
   English Muffin Bread   18
   Lovely Oatmeal Bread   19
   Easy Multigrain Bread   20

Fruit and Vegetable Bread   21

   Fragrant Orange Bread   21
   Strawberry Shortcake Bread   22
   Banana Sour Cream Bread   23
   Pineapple Coconut Bread   24
   Fruit Syrup Bread   25
   Lemon-Lime Blueberry Bread   26
   Cranberry Yogurt Bread   27
   Peaches and Cream Bread   28
   Cinnamon and Raisin Pumpernickel Bread   29
   Zucchini and Berries Loaf   30
   Yeasted Carrot Bread   31
   Zucchini Rye Bread   32

Savory Onion Bread	33
Confetti Bread	34

Spice And Herb Breads — 35

Herbed Italian Style Bread	35
Fragrant Herb Bread	36
Stew Bread	37
Rosemary Bread	38
Basil and Sun-Dried Dinner Loaf	39
Spicy Cajun Bread	40
Sweet and Chilli Pumpernickel Bread	41
Cracked Black Pepper Bread	42
Potato and Rosemary Loaf	43
Cinnamon Bread	44
Simple Garlic Bread	45

Cheese Bread — 46

Cheddar Cheese Basil Bread	46
Herb and Parmesan Cheese Loaf	47
Olive Cheese Bread	48
Beer and Cheese Bread	49
Blue Cheese Onion Bread	50
Cheese Loaf	51
Double Cheese Bread	52
Three Cheese Bread	53
Spinach and Feta Whole Wheat Bread	54
Mozzarella and Salami Bread	55
Cheese Swirl Loaf	56
Chile Cheese Bacon Bread	57
Italian Parmesan Bread	58
Lava Cheese and Onion Bread	59
Feta Oregano Bread	60

Sweet Bread — 61

Chocolate Chip Peanut Butter Banana Bread	*61*
Portuguese Sweet Bread	*62*
Sour Cream Maple Bread	*63*
Chocolate Amish Bread	*64*
Barmbrack Bread	*65*
Gooey Cinnamon Roll	*66*
Crusty Honey Bread	*67*
Portuguese Sweet Bread	*68*
Honey Granola Bread	*69*
Custard Filled Dinner Rolls	*70*
Vanilla Almond Milk Bread	*71*
Chocolate Oatmeal Banana Bread	*72*
Pumpkin Coconut Bread	*73*
Chocolate Chip Bread	*74*

Gluten-Free Bread — **75**

Gluten-Free White Bread	*75*
Brown Rice Bread	*76*
Brown Rice and Cranberry Bread	*77*
Gluten-Free Peasant Bread	*78*
Gluten-Free Hawaiian Loaf	*79*
Vegan Gluten-Free Bread	*80*

Sourdough Breads — **81**

Sourdough Starter	*81*
Oat Sourdough Loaf	*82*
Whole-Wheat Sourdough Bread	*83*
Basic Sourdough Loaf	*84*
Multigrain Sourdough Bread	*85*
Sourdough Milk Bread	*86*
Sourdough Beer Bread	*87*
Crusty Sourdough Bread	*88*
Herb Sourdough	*89*

ERITAGE OF FOOD: A FAMILY GATHERING 90

About the Author 91

INTRODUCTION

Hamilton Beach Bread Machine Cookbook for beginners: The Best, Easy, Gluten-Free and Foolproof recipes for your Hamilton Beach Bread Machine

There is nothing better than the exquisite and delicious aroma of freshly baked bread that fills the kitchen.

However, baking bread from scratch is a slow, challenging, and complicated process. Having to knead, taste, and bake the dough can take hours, and creating the perfect and crispy increase can take years to master.

Everyone loves the taste and smell of the fresh bread, but not the time it takes to bake it. Making bread should be simple… and now it is.

The Hamilton Beach Bread machine is now the hot item in the kitchen because it takes the work out of making homemade bread. Even better, the Hamilton Beach Bread Machine Cookbook takes the mystery out of the bread machine and brings you easy-to-use recipes. With more than 100 recipes that use easy-to-find ingredients and require minimal work, this Hamilton Beach bread machine cookbook will set you up for baking success.

Put down the dough and pick up this book. The Hamilton Beach Bread Machine Cookbook is the first and only collection of easy, hassle-free recipes that give you delicious homemade loaves of bread every time.

Recipes include:

- Every Day Bread
- Classic favorites
- Rustic bread
- Sweet doughs
- Coffeecakes
- Fruit Bread
- Herb and Spice Bread
- Whole Wheat Bread
- Gluten-Free Bread
- Nut Bread

- Cheese Bread
- Sweet Roll
- Chocolate Bread

There's nothing than the taste and smell of homemade bread!

Enjoy the Hamilton Beach Bread Machine Cookbook!

Enjoy the Homemade Bread recipes!

Basic Bread

Regular Soft White Loaf
PREP: 10 MINUTES
Size: **1.5 pounds**

Ingredients:
- 3 cups + 2 tbsp all-purpose flour
- 1 cup water
- 2 tbsp oil
- 2 tbsp sugar
- 3 tbsp milk
- 1 tbsp instant yeast

Directions:
1. **Preparing the Ingredients.** Place all ingredients in the bread pan in the liquid-dry-yeast layering.
   Put the pan in the Hamilton Beach bread machine.
2. **Select the Bake cycle.** Choose White Bread.
   Press start and wait until the loaf is cooked. The machine will automatically start the keep warm mode after the bread is complete. Let it stay in that mode for about 10 minutes before unplugging.
   Remove the pan and let it cool down for about 10 minutes.

Healthy Bran Bread

PREP: 10 MINUTES
Size: 1.5 pounds

Ingredients:
- 1⅛ cups milk, at 80°F to 90°F
- 2¼ tablespoons melted butter, cooled
- 3 tablespoons sugar
- 1½ teaspoons salt
- ⅓ cup wheat bran
- 2⅔ cups white bread flour
- 1½ teaspoon bread machine or instant yeast

Directions:

1. **Preparing the Ingredients.** Place the ingredients in your Hamilton Beach bread machine.

2. **Select the Bake cycle.** Program the machine White bread, select light or medium crust, and press Start. When the loaf is done, remove the bucket from the machine. Let the loaf cool for 5 minutes. Gently shake the bucket to remove the loaf, and turn it out onto a rack to cool.

Pumpernickel Bread Loaf

PREP: 10 MINUTES
Size: 1.5 pounds

Ingredients:
- 1 cup bread flour
- ⅓ cup rye flour
- ¾ cup wheat flour
- 5/6 cup lukewarm water
- 2 tbsp cocoa powder
- 6 tbsp oil
- ½ tbsp salt
- 1 tbsp instant yeast
- ½ cup molasses

Directions:

1. **Preparing the Ingredients.** In a bowl, combine the water, molasses, salt, and oil. Stir until incorporated.
   Place all ingredients in the bread pan in the liquid-dry-yeast layering.
   Put the pan in the Hamilton Beach bread machine.
2. **Select the Bake cycle.** Choose whole wheat loaf.
   Press start and wait until the loaf is cooked. The machine will automatically start the keep warm mode after the bread is complete. Let it stay in that mode for about 10 minutes before unplugging.
   Remove the pan and let it cool down for about 10 minutes.

Soft Rye Bread

PREP: 10 MINUTES
Size: 1.5 pounds

Ingredients:

2 cups all-purpose or bread flour
2 ¾ cup rye flour
2 tbsp cocoa powder
½ cup cornmeal
1 tbsp instant yeast
¼ cup corn or olive oil
3 tbsp honey
1½ cup lukewarm water
1 tsp salt

Directions:

1. **Preparing the Ingredients.** In a bowl, combine all the dry ingredients, except for yeast. In another bowl, dissolve the honey in the water.
   Place all ingredients in the bread pan in the liquid-dry-yeast layering.
   Put the pan in the Hamilton Beach bread machine.
2. **Select the Bake cycle.** Choose White bread.
   Press start and wait until the loaf is cooked. The machine will automatically start the keep warm mode after the bread is complete. Let it stay in that mode for about 10 minutes before unplugging.
   Remove the pan and let it cool down for about 10 minutes.

Soft Egg Bread
PREP: 10 MINUTES
Size: 1.5 pounds

Ingredients:
- ¾ cup milk, at 80°F to 90°F
- ¼ cup melted butter, cooled
- 2 eggs, at room temperature
- ¼ cup sugar
- 1½ teaspoons salt
- 3 cups white bread flour
- 1 teaspoon bread machine or instant yeast

Directions:
1. **Preparing the Ingredients.** Place the ingredients in your Hamilton Beach bread machine.
2. **Select the Bake cycle.** Program the machine for White bread, select light or medium crust, and press Start. When the loaf is done, remove the bucket from the machine. Let the loaf cool for 5 minutes.
Gently shake the bucket to remove the loaf, and turn it out onto a rack to cool.

Golden Raisin Bread
PREP: 10 MINUTES
Size: 1.5 pounds

Ingredients:
- 1⅛ cups milk, at 80°F to 90°F
- 1½ tablespoons melted butter, cooled
- 2 tablespoons sugar
- 1 teaspoon salt
- ¾ teaspoon ground cinnamon
- 3 cups white bread flour
- 1½ teaspoons bread machine or instant yeast
- ¾ cup golden raisins

Directions:
1. **Preparing the Ingredients.** Place the ingredients, except the raisins, in your Hamilton Beach bread machine.
2. **Select the Bake cycle.** Program the machine for White or Sweet bread, select light or medium crust, and press Start.
   Add the raisins at the raisin/nut signal. When the loaf is done, remove the bucket from the machine. Let the loaf cool for 5 minutes.
   Gently shake the bucket to remove the loaf, and turn it out onto a rack to cool.

Whole Wheat Soda Bread

PREP: 10 MINUTES
Size: 1.5 pounds

Ingredients:
- 1½ cups all purpose flour
- 2 cups bread flour
- 1 tsp sugar
- 1 tsp salt
- 2 cups buttermilk
- 1½ tsp olive oil
- ½ cup evaporated or full cream milk
- 1 tsp baking soda

Directions:
1. **Preparing the Ingredients.** Combine all the dry ingredients. Mix all the wet ingredients. Place in the bread pan in the liquid-dry layering.
Put the pan in the Hamilton Beach bread machine.
Set the loaf size and choose medium for the crust color.
2. **Select the Bake cycle.** Press the menu and choose Rapid Whole Wheat. This bread has no yeast and does not need the rising and proofing time. Press Start. Set the rapid bake time to 45 minutes.
Remove the pan from the bread machine immediately. Cool in the pan completely.

Golden Corn Bread

PREP: 10 MINUTES
Size: 2 pounds

Ingredients:
- 1 cup buttermilk, at 80°F to 90°F
- ¼ cup melted butter, cooled
- 2 eggs, at room temperature
- 1⅓ cups all-purpose flour
- 1 cup cornmeal
- ¼ cup sugar
- 1 tablespoon baking powder
- 1 teaspoon salt

Directions:
1. **Preparing the Ingredients.** Place the buttermilk, butter, and eggs in your Hamilton Beach bread machine.
2. **Select the Bake cycle.** Program the machine for Rapid White bread and press Start. While the wet ingredients are mixing, stir together the flour, cornmeal, sugar, baking powder, and salt in a small bowl.
After the first fast mixing is done and the machine signals, add the dry ingredients. When the loaf is done, remove the bucket from the machine. Let the loaf cool for 5 minutes. Gently shake the bucket to remove the loaf, and turn it out onto a rack to cool.

Peasant Bread

PREP: 10 MINUTES
Size: 1.5 pounds

Ingredients:
- 3½ cups bread or all-purpose four
- 1 tbsp instant yeast
- 1½ cups lukewarm water
- 1 tsp salt
- 1 tbsp sugar

Directions:
1. **Preparing the Ingredients.** Combine the yeast, sugar, and water. Set aside for five minutes to bloom.
    Place the bloomed yeast and the rest of the ingredients in the bread pan. Set it in the bread machine.
2. **Select the Bake cycle.** Set the loaf size and color to blank. Choose White bread. Press Start. The dough will take at least about an hour and a half to rise, but do not complete it.
    Press stop halfway into the cycle and reset the bread machine. This time choose White Bread cycle and medium to dark crust.
    Press start and wait until the loaf is cooked. The machine will automatically start the keep warm mode after the bread is complete. Let it stay in that mode for about 10 minutes before unplugging.
    Remove the pan and let it cool down for about 10 minutes.

English Muffin Bread

PREP: 10 MINUTES
Size: 1.5 pounds

Ingredients:
- 1¼ cups buttermilk, at 80°F to 90°F
- 1½ tablespoons melted butter, cooled
- 1½ tablespoons sugar
- 1⅛ teaspoons salt
- ⅓ teaspoon baking powder
- 2⅔ cups white bread flour
- 1⅔ teaspoons bread machine or instant yeast

Directions:
1. **Preparing the Ingredients.** Place the ingredients in your Hamilton Beach bread machine.
2. **Select the Bake cycle.** Program the machine for White bread, select light or medium crust, and press Start.
   When the loaf is done, remove the bucket from the machine. Let the loaf cool for 5 minutes. Gently shake the bucket to remove the loaf, and turn it out onto a rack to cool.

Lovely Oatmeal Bread
PREP: 10 MINUTES
Size: 1.5 pounds

Ingredients:
- 1⅛ cups water, at 80°F to 90°F
- 3 tablespoons melted butter, cooled
- 3 tablespoons sugar
- 1½ teaspoons salt
- 1 cup quick oats
- 2¼ cups white bread flour
- 1½ teaspoons bread machine or instant yeast

Directions:
1. **Preparing the Ingredients.** Place the ingredients in your Hamilton Beach bread machine.
2. **Select the Bake cycle.** Program the machine for White bread, select light or medium crust, and press Start.
   When the loaf is done, remove the bucket from the machine. Let the loaf cool for 5 minutes. Gently shake the bucket to remove the loaf, and turn it out onto a rack to cool.

Easy Multigrain Bread

PREP: 10 MINUTES
Size: 1.5 pounds

Ingredients:
1¼ cup bread flour or whole wheat
1 cup rye flour
¾ cup multi-grain cereal
1 tsp salt
1½ tsp instant dry yeast
2 tbsp sugar
2 tbsp powdered milk
1⅓ cup lukewarm milk

Directions:
1. **Preparing the Ingredients.** Place the cereal in the food processor and grind finely. Measure ¾ cup.
   Place all ingredients in the bread pan in the liquid-dry-yeast layering, including cereal. Put the pan in the Hamilton Beach bread machine.
2. **Select the Bake cycle.** Choose Whole Wheat.
   Press start and wait until the loaf is cooked. The machine will automatically start the keep warm mode after the bread is complete. Let it stay in that mode for about 10 minutes before unplugging.
   Remove the pan and let it cool down for about 10 minutes.

Fruit and Vegetable Bread

Fragrant Orange Bread
PREP: 10 MINUTES
Size: 1.5 pounds

Ingredients:
1 cup milk, at 80°F to 90°F
3 tablespoons freshly squeezed orange juice, at room temperature
3 tablespoons sugar
1 tablespoon melted butter, cooled
1 teaspoon salt
3 cups white bread flour
Zest of 1 orange
1¼ teaspoons bread machine or instant yeast

Directions:
1. **Preparing the Ingredients.** Place the ingredients in your Hamilton Beach bread machine.
2. **Select the Bake cycle.** Program the machine for White bread, select light or medium crust, and press Start. When the loaf is done, remove the bucket from the machine. Let the loaf cool for 5 minutes. Gently shake the bucket to remove the loaf, and turn it out onto a rack to cool.

Strawberry Shortcake Bread
PREP: 10 MINUTES
Size: 1.5 pounds

Ingredients:
1⅛ cups milk, at 80°F to 90°F
3 tablespoons melted butter, cooled
3 tablespoons sugar
1½ teaspoons salt
¾ cup sliced fresh strawberries
1 cup quick oats
2¼ cups white bread flour
1½ teaspoons bread machine or instant yeast

Directions:
1. **Preparing the Ingredients.** Place the ingredients in your Hamilton Beach bread machine.
2. **Select the Bake cycle.** Program the machine for White bread, select light or medium crust, and press Start. When the loaf is done, remove the bucket from the machine. Let the loaf cool for 5 minutes. Gently shake the bucket to remove the loaf, and turn it out onto a rack to cool.

Banana Sour Cream Bread

PREP: 10 MINUTES
Size: 1.5 pounds

Ingredients:
2¼ cups all-purpose flour
1½ cup white sugar
¼ cup butter, melted
1 tsp ground cinnamon
3 overripe bananas, mashed
2 cups sour cream
1 tsp vanilla extract
pinch of salt
2 tsp baking soda
2 eggs
2 tbsp sugar mix with ½ tsp cinnamon

Directions:
1. **Preparing the Ingredients.** Place all ingredients, except sugar and cinnamon mix, in the bread pan in the liquid-dry-yeast layering. Put the pan in the Hamilton Beach bread machine.
2. **Select the Bake cycle.** Set to rapid White bread. Press Start.
   Before the baking starts, pause the machine and sprinkle on the cinnamon sugar. Resume. Wait until the loaf is cooked. The machine will automatically start the keep warm mode after the bread is complete. Let it stay in that mode for about 10 minutes before unplugging.
   Remove the pan and let it cool down for about 10 minutes.
   Herbed and Spiced Bread

Pineapple Coconut Bread

PREP: 10 MINUTES
Size: 2 pounds

Ingredients:
6 tablespoons butter, at room temperature
2 eggs, at room temperature
½ cup coconut milk, at room temperature
½ cup pineapple juice, at room temperature
1 cup sugar
1½ teaspoons coconut extract
2 cups all-purpose flour
¾ cup shredded sweetened coconut
1 teaspoon baking powder
½ teaspoon salt

Directions:
1. **Preparing the Ingredients.** Place the butter, eggs, coconut milk, pineapple juice, sugar, and coconut extract in your Hamilton Beach bread machine.
2. **Select the Bake cycle.** Program the machine for Rapid bread and press Start. While the wet ingredients are mixing, stir together the flour, coconut, baking powder, and salt in a small bowl. After the first fast mixing is done and the machine signals, add the dry ingredients. When the loaf is done, remove the bucket from the machine. Let the loaf cool for 5 minutes. Gently shake the bucket to remove the loaf, and turn it out onto a rack to cool.

Fruit Syrup Bread

PREP: 10 MINUTES
Size: 1.5 pounds

Ingredients:
3⅔ cups whole wheat flour
1½ tsp instant yeast
¼ cup unsalted butter, melted
1 cup lukewarm water
2 tbsp sugar
¼ cup rolled oats
½ tsp salt
½ cup of syrup from preserved fruit

Directions:
1. **Preparing the Ingredients.** Combine the syrup and ½ cup water. Heat until lukewarm. Add more water to exactly 1 cup water.
   Place all the ingredients, except for the rolled oats and butter, in a liquid-dry-yeast layering.
   Put the pan in the Hamilton Beach bread machine.
   Load the rolled oats in the automatic dispenser.
2. **Select the Bake cycle.** Choose whole wheat loaf.
   Press start and wait until the loaf is cooked.
   Brush the top with butter once cooked.
   The machine will automatically start the keep warm mode after the bread is complete.
   Let it stay in that mode for about 10 minutes before unplugging.
   Remove the pan and let it cool down for about 10 minutes.

Lemon-Lime Blueberry Bread

PREP: 10 MINUTES
Size: 1.5 pounds

Ingredients:
¾ cup plain yogurt, at room temperature
½ cup water, at 80°F to 90°F
3 tablespoons honey
1 tablespoon melted butter, cooled
1½ teaspoons salt
½ teaspoon lemon extract
1 teaspoon lime zest
1 cup dried blueberries
3 cups white bread flour
2¼ teaspoons bread machine or instant yeast

Directions:
1. **Preparing the Ingredients.** Place the ingredients in your Hamilton Beach bread machine.
2. **Select the Bake cycle.** Program the machine for White bread, select light or medium crust, and press Start.
   When the loaf is done, remove the bucket from the machine.
   Let the loaf cool for 5 minutes.
   Gently shake the bucket to remove the loaf, and turn it out onto a rack to cool.

Cranberry Yogurt Bread

PREP: 10 MINUTES
Size: 1.5 pounds

Ingredients:
3 cups + 2 tbsp bread or all-purpose flour
½ cup lukewarm water
1 tbsp olive or coconut oil
1 tbsp orange or lemon essential oil
3 tbsp sugar
¾ cup yogurt
2 tsp instant yeast
1 cup dried cried cranberries
½ cup raisins

Directions:
1. **Preparing the Ingredients.** Place all ingredients, except cranberries and raisins, in the bread pan in the liquid-dry-yeast layering.
Put the pan in the Hamilton Beach bread machine.
Load the fruits in the automatic dispenser.
2. **Select the Bake cycle.** Choose White bread.
Press start and wait until the loaf is cooked. The machine will automatically start the keep warm mode after the bread is complete. Let it stay in that mode for about 10 minutes before unplugging.
Remove the pan and let it cool down for about 10 minutes.

Peaches and Cream Bread
PREP: 10 MINUTES
Size: 1.5 pounds

Ingredients:
¾ cup canned peaches, drained and chopped
⅓ cup heavy whipping cream, at 80°F to 90°F
1 egg, at room temperature
1 tablespoon melted butter, cooled
2¼ tablespoons sugar
1⅛ teaspoons salt
⅓ teaspoon ground cinnamon
⅛ teaspoon ground nutmeg
⅓ cup whole-wheat flour
2⅔ cups white bread flour
1⅛ teaspoons bread machine or instant yeast

Directions:
1. **Preparing the Ingredients.** Place the ingredients in your Hamilton Beach bread machine.
2. **Select the Bake cycle.** Program the machine for White bread, select light or medium crust, and press Start.
   When the loaf is done, remove the bucket from the machine.
   Let the loaf cool for 5 minutes.
   Gently shake the bucket to remove the loaf, and turn it out onto a rack to cool.

Cinnamon and Raisin Pumpernickel Bread

PREP: 10 MINUTES
Size: 1.5 pounds

Ingredients:
1 cup bread flour
⅓ cup rye flour
¾ cup wheat flour
5/6 cup lukewarm water
2 tbsp cocoa powder
6 tbsp oil or melted shortening
½ tbsp salt
1 tbsp instant yeast
½ cup molasses
¼ cup honey
1½ tbsp cinnamon
1 cup raisins

Directions:
1. **Preparing the Ingredients.** In a bowl, combine the water, molasses, salt, and oil. Stir until incorporated.
   Place all ingredients, except raisins, in the bread pan in the liquid-dry-yeast layering. Put the pan in the Hamilton Beach bread machine.
   Load the raisins in the automatic dispenser
2. **Select the Bake cycle.** Choose Whole Wheat loaf.
   Press start and wait until the loaf is cooked. The machine will automatically start the keep warm mode after the bread is complete. Let it stay in that mode for about 10 minutes before unplugging.
   Remove the pan and let it cool down for about 10 minutes.

Zucchini and Berries Loaf

PREP: 1 HOUR
Size: 1.5 pounds

Ingredients:
2¼ cups flour
3 eggs, whisked lightly
1 ⅔ cups sugar
2 tsp vanilla
¾ cup vegetable oil
¾ tsp baking powder
pinch of baking soda
¼ tsp salt
2 tsp cinnamon
1½ cup blueberries
1½ cup shredded zucchini

Directions:
1. **Preparing the Ingredients.** Mix the dry and wet ingredients in separate bowls.
   Place all ingredients, except the berries, in the bread pan in the liquid-dry-yeast-zucchini layering.
   Put the pan in the Hamilton Beach bread machine.
   Load the berries in the automatic dispenser.
2. **Select the Bake cycle.** Set to Rapid White bake for 1 hour. Press Start.
   5 minutes into the cycle, add the berries.
   Wait until the loaf is cooked. The machine will automatically start the keep warm mode after the bread is complete. Let it stay in that mode for about 10 minutes before unplugging.
   Remove the pan and let it cool down for about 10 minutes.

Yeasted Carrot Bread

PREP: 10 MINUTES
Size: 1.5 pounds

Ingredients:
¾ cup milk, at 80°F to 90°F
3 tablespoons melted butter, cooled
1 tablespoon honey
1½ cups shredded carrot
¾ teaspoon ground nutmeg
½ teaspoon salt
3 cups white bread flour
2¼ teaspoons bread machine or active dry yeast

Directions:
1. **Preparing the Ingredients.** Place the ingredients in your Hamilton Beach bread machine.
2. **Select the Bake cycle.** Program the machine for Rapid bread and press Start.
   When the loaf is done, remove the bucket from the machine.
   Let the loaf cool for 5 minutes.
   Gently shake the bucket to remove the loaf, and turn it out onto a rack to cool.

Zucchini Rye Bread

PREP: 10 MINUTES
Size: 1.5 pounds

Ingredients:
2 cups all-purpose or bread flour
2¾ cup rye flour
2 tbsp cocoa powder
½ cup cornmeal
1 tbsp instant yeast
¼ cup olive oil
3 tbsp molasses or honey
1½ cup lukewarm water
1 tsp salt
1½ cup zucchini, shredded

Directions:
1. **Preparing the Ingredients.** Dry the shredded zucchini but placing it in a towel and wringing it to remove excess moisture.
   Place all the ingredients in the liquid-zucchini-flour-yeast layering.
   Put the pan in the Hamilton Beach bread machine.
2. **Select the Bake cycle.** Choose White bread and medium crust.
   Press start and wait until the loaf is cooked. The machine will automatically start the keep warm mode after the bread is complete. Let it stay in that mode for about 10 minutes before unplugging.
   Remove the pan and let it cool down for about 10 minutes

Savory Onion Bread
PREP: 10 MINUTES
Size: 1.5 pounds

Ingredients:
1 cup water, at 80°F to 90°F
3 tablespoons melted butter, cooled
1½ tablespoons sugar
1⅛ teaspoons salt
3 tablespoons dried minced onion
1½ tablespoons chopped fresh chives
3 cups plus 2 tablespoons white bread flour
1⅔ teaspoons bread machine or instant yeast

Directions:
1. **Preparing the Ingredients.** Place the ingredients in your Hamilton Beach bread machine.
2. **Select the Bake cycle.** Program the machine for White bread, select light or medium crust, and press Start.
   When the loaf is done, remove the bucket from the machine.
   Let the loaf cool for 5 minutes.
   Gently shake the bucket to remove the loaf, and turn it out onto a rack to cool.

Confetti Bread

PREP: 10 MINUTES
Size: 1.5 pounds

Ingredients:
½ cup milk, at 80°F to 90°F
3 tablespoons water, at 80°F to 90°F
1 tablespoon melted butter, cooled
1 teaspoon white vinegar
2 tablespoons sugar
1 teaspoon salt
2 tablespoons grated Parmesan cheese
½ cup quick oats
2½ cups white bread flour
1½ teaspoons bread machine or instant yeast
½ cup finely chopped zucchini
¼ cup finely chopped yellow bell pepper
¼ cup finely chopped red bell pepper
2 tablespoons chopped chives

Directions:
1. **Preparing the Ingredients**. Place the ingredients, except the vegetables, in your Hamilton Beach bread machine.
   Select the Bake cycle. Program the machine for White bread, select light or medium crust, and press Start.
   When the machine signals, add the chopped vegetables; if your machine has no signal, add the vegetables just before the second kneading is finished.
   When the loaf is done, remove the bucket from the machine.
   Let the loaf cool for 5 minutes.
   Gently shake the bucket to remove the loaf, and turn it out onto a rack to cool.

Spice And Herb Breads

Herbed Italian Style Bread
PREP: 10 MINUTES
Size: 1.5 pounds

Ingredients:
4 cups all purpose flour
2 tbsp instant yeast
1 tbsp brown sugar
1⅓ cup lukewarm water
1 tsp salt
1½ tsp corn or olive oil
2 tbsp cornmeal or bread crumbs
egg wash
1 tsp dried rosemary
1 tsp dried oregano
2 tbsp dried basil
pinch of cayenne pepper

Directions:
1. **Preparing the Ingredients**: Place all ingredients, except egg wash and cornmeal, in the bread pan in the liquid-dry-yeast layering.
   Put the pan in the Hamilton Beach bread machine.
2. **Select the Bake cycle.** Choose White bread. Press Start.
   Prior to the start of the baking process, pause the machine. Brush with egg wash and sprinkle with cornmeal.
   Resume and wait until the loaf is cooked. The machine will automatically start the keep warm mode after the bread is complete. Let it stay in that mode for about 10 minutes before unplugging.
   Remove the pan and let it cool down for about 10 minutes.

Fragrant Herb Bread

PREP: 10 MINUTES
Size: 1.5 pounds

Ingredients:

1⅛ cups water, at 80°F to 90°F
1½ tablespoons melted butter, cooled
1½ tablespoons sugar
1 teaspoon salt
3 tablespoons skim milk powder
1 teaspoon dried thyme
1 teaspoon dried chives
1 teaspoon dried oregano
3 cups white bread flour
1¼ teaspoons bread machine or instant yeast

Directions:
1. **Preparing the Ingredients.** Place the ingredients in your Hamilton Beach bread machine.
2. **Select the Bake cycle.** Program the machine for White bread, select light or medium crust, and press Start.
   When the loaf is done, remove the bucket from the machine.
   Let the loaf cool for 5 minutes.
   Gently shake the bucket to remove the loaf, and turn it out onto a rack to cool.

Stew Bread

PREP: 10 MINUTES
Size: 1.5 pounds

Ingredients:
4 cups bread flour
1 cup lukewarm water
2½ tsp instant yeast
3 tbsp milk
½ cup sugar
2 eggs
1/8 cup butter
1/8 cup shortening
1 tsp dried sage
1 tsp dried parsley
½ tsp nutmeg
2 tsp celery seed
1 tsp onion powder

Directions:
1. **Preparing the Ingredients.** Place all ingredients in the bread pan in the liquid-dry-yeast layering.
   Put the pan in the Hamilton Beach bread machine.
2. **Select the Bake cycle.** Choose White bread.
   Press start and wait until the loaf is cooked. The machine will automatically start the keep warm mode after the bread is complete. Let it stay in that mode for about 10 minutes before unplugging.
   Remove the pan and let it cool down for about 10 minutes.

Rosemary Bread

PREP: 10 MINUTES
Size: 1.5 pounds

Ingredients:
1¼ cups water, at 80°F to 90°F
2½ tablespoons melted butter, cooled
1 tablespoon sugar
1½ teaspoons salt
1½ tablespoons finely chopped fresh rosemary
3 cups white bread flour
2 teaspoons bread machine or instant yeast

Directions:
1. **Preparing the Ingredients.** Place the ingredients in your Hamilton Beach bread machine.
2. **Select the Bake cycle.** Program the machine for White bread, select light or medium crust, and press Start.
   When the loaf is done, remove the bucket from the machine.
   Let the loaf cool for 5 minutes.
   Gently shake the bucket to remove the loaf, and turn it out onto a rack to cool.

Basil and Sun-Dried Dinner Loaf

PREP: 10 MINUTES
Size: 1.5 pounds

Ingredients:
3⅔ bread flour
⅓ cup quinoa
1 tbsp active yeast
1 cup lukewarm water
3 tbsp light brown sugar
3 tbsp butter, softened
1 tbsp coconut or olive oil
1 tsp salt
2 tbsp milk powder
1 egg
1 cup sun dried tomatoes
boiling water
1 tsp dried basil

Directions:
1. **Preparing the Ingredients.** Pour boiled water over the tomatoes and let sit for 5 minutes. Drain the tomatoes and discard the water. Dry with paper towel and chop into tiny bits.
   Place all ingredients, except tomatoes in the bread pan in the liquid-dry-yeast layering. Put the pan in the Hamilton Beach bread machine.
   Load the tomatoes into the automatic dispenser. If you do not have one, most bread machines will have a notification alarm on when to add extra ingredients.
2. **Select the Bake cycle.** Choose White bread.
   Press start and wait until the loaf is cooked. The machine will automatically start the keep warm mode after the bread is complete. Let it stay in that mode for about 10 minutes before unplugging.
   Finish the baking cycle.

Spicy Cajun Bread

PREP: 10 MINUTES
Size: 1.5 pounds

Ingredients:
1⅛ cups water, at 80°F to 90°F
1½ tablespoons melted butter, cooled
1 tablespoon tomato paste
1½ tablespoons sugar
1½ teaspoons salt
3 tablespoons skim milk powder
¾ tablespoon Cajun seasoning
¼ teaspoon onion powder
3 cups white bread flour
1¼ teaspoons bread machine or instant yeast

Directions:
1. **Preparing the Ingredients.** Place the ingredients in your Hamilton Beach bread machine as recommended by the manufacturer.
2. **Select the Bake cycle.** Program the machine for Basic/White bread, select light or medium crust, and press Start.
   When the loaf is done, remove the bucket from the machine.
   Let the loaf cool for 5 minutes.
   Gently shake the bucket to remove the loaf, and turn it out onto a rack to cool.

Sweet and Chilli Pumpernickel Bread

PREP: 10 MINUTES
Size: 1.5 pounds

Ingredients:
1 cup bread flour
⅓ cup rye flour
¾ cup wheat flour
5/6 cup lukewarm water
2 tbsp cocoa powder
6 tbsp oil or melted shortening
½ tbsp salt
1 tbsp instant yeast
½ cup molasses
¼ cup honey
1 tsp chilli powder
½ tsp garlic powder
½ tsp onion powder
1 medium onion, minced, optional

Directions:
1. **Preparing the Ingredients.** In a bowl, combine the water, molasses, salt, and oil. Stir until incorporated.
   Place all ingredients in the bread pan in the liquid-dry-yeast layering.
   Put the pan in the Hamilton Beach bread machine.
2. **Select the Bake cycle.** Choose Whole Wheat loaf.
   Press start and wait until the loaf is cooked. The machine will automatically start the keep warm mode after the bread is complete. Let it stay in that mode for about 10 minutes before unplugging.
   Remove the pan and let it cool down for about 10 minutes.

Cracked Black Pepper Bread

PREP: 10 MINUTES
Size: 1.5 pounds

Ingredients:
1⅛ cups water, at 80°F to 90°F
1½ tablespoons melted butter, cooled
1½ tablespoons sugar
1 teaspoon salt
3 tablespoons skim milk powder
1½ tablespoons minced chives
¾ teaspoon garlic powder
¾ teaspoon freshly cracked black pepper
3 cups white bread flour
1¼ teaspoons bread machine or instant yeast

Directions:
1. **Preparing the Ingredients.** Place the ingredients in your Hamilton Beach bread machine
2. **Select the Bake cycle.** Program the machine for White bread, select light or medium crust, and press Start.
   When the loaf is done, remove the bucket from the machine.
   Let the loaf cool for 5 minutes.
   Gently shake the bucket to remove the loaf, and turn it out onto a rack to cool.

Potato and Rosemary Loaf

PREP: 10 MINUTES
Size: 1.5 pounds

Ingredients:
2 7/8 cups all purpose flour
1 cup warm milk
3 tbsp sugar
1 tsp salt
1½ tsp instant yeast
3 tbsp oil
½ half cup mashed potato (unsalted)
1 tsp rosemary

Directions:

1. **Preparing the Ingredients.** In a bowl, combine the mashed potato and ¼ cup milk. Cool until lukewarm.
   Place the rest of the milk in the bread pan. Sprinkle the yeast and 1 tbsp of sugar. Stir to mix and wait for the yeast to bloom for about 5 minutes.
   Add the lukewarm potato mixture, the oil and the rest of the dry ingredients. Close the lid.
   Put the pan in the Hamilton Beach bread machine.
2. **Select the Bake cycle.** Choose White bread.
   Press start and wait until the loaf is cooked. The machine will automatically start the keep warm mode after the bread is complete. Let it stay in that mode for about 10 minutes before unplugging.
   Remove the pan and let it cool down for about 10 minutes.

Cinnamon Bread

PREP: 10 MINUTES
Size: 1.5 pounds

Ingredients:
1 cup milk, at 80°F to 90°F
1 egg, at room temperature
¼ cup melted butter, cooled
½ cup sugar
½ teaspoon salt
1½ teaspoons ground cinnamon
3 cups white bread flour
2 teaspoons bread machine or active dry yeast

Directions:
1. **Preparing the Ingredients.** Place the ingredients in your Hamilton Beach bread machine.
2. **Select the Bake cycle.** Program the machine for White bread, select light or medium crust, and press Start.
   When the loaf is done, remove the bucket from the machine.
   Let the loaf cool for 5 minutes.
   Gently shake the bucket to remove the loaf, and turn it out onto a rack to cool.

Simple Garlic Bread
PREP: 10 MINUTES
Size: 1.5 pounds

Ingredients:
1 cup milk, at 70°F to 80°F
1½ tablespoons melted butter, cooled
1 tablespoon sugar
1½ teaspoons salt
2 teaspoons garlic powder
2 teaspoons chopped fresh parsley
3 cups white bread flour
1¾ teaspoons bread machine or instant yeast

Directions:
1. **Preparing the Ingredients.** Place the ingredients in your Hamilton Beach bread machine.
2. **Select the Bake cycle.** Program the machine for White bread, select light or medium crust, and press Start.
   When the loaf is done, remove the bucket from the machine.
   Let the loaf cool for 5 minutes.
   Gently shake the bucket to remove the loaf, and turn it out onto a rack to cool.

Cheese Bread

Cheddar Cheese Basil Bread
PREP: 10 MINUTES
Size: 1.5 pounds

Ingredients:
1 cup milk, at 80°F to 90°F
1 tablespoon melted butter, cooled
1 tablespoon sugar
1 teaspoon dried basil
¾ cup (3 ounces) shredded sharp Cheddar cheese
¾ teaspoon salt
3 cups white bread flour
1½ teaspoons bread machine or active dry yeast

Directions:
1. **Preparing the Ingredients.** Place the ingredients in your Hamilton Beach bread machine.
2. **Select the Bake cycle.** Program the machine for White bread, select light or medium crust, and press Start.
   When the loaf is done, remove the bucket from the machine.
   Let the loaf cool for 5 minutes.
   Gently shake the bucket to remove the loaf, and turn it out onto a rack to cool.

Herb and Parmesan Cheese Loaf

PREP: 10 MINUTES
Size: 1.5 pounds

Ingredients:
3 cups + 2 tbsp all-purpose flour
1 cup water
2 tbsp oil
2 tbsp sugar
3 tbsp milk
1 tbsp instant yeast
1 tsp garlic powder
5 tbsp parmesan cheese
1 tbsp fresh basil
1 tbsp fresh oregano
1 tbsp fresh chives or rosemary

Directions:

1. **Preparing the Ingredients.** Place all ingredients in the bread pan in the liquid-cheese and herb-dry-yeast layering.
   Put the pan in the Hamilton Beach bread machine.
2. **Select the Bake cycle.** Choose White bread.
   Press start and wait until the loaf is cooked. The machine will automatically start the keep warm mode after the bread is complete. Let it stay in that mode for about 10 minutes before unplugging.
   Remove the pan and let it cool down for about 10 minutes.

Olive Cheese Bread

PREP: 10 MINUTES
Size: 1.5 pounds

Ingredients:
1 cup milk, at 80°F to 90°F
1½ tablespoons melted butter, cooled
1 teaspoon minced garlic
1½ tablespoons sugar
1 teaspoon salt
3 cups white bread flour
¾ cup (3 ounces) shredded Swiss cheese
1 teaspoon bread machine or instant yeast
⅓ cup chopped black olives

Directions:
1. **Preparing the Ingredients.** Place the ingredients in your Hamilton Beach bread machine, tossing the flour with the cheese first.
2. **Select the Bake cycle.** Program the machine for White bread, select light or medium crust, and press Start.
   When the loaf is done, remove the bucket from the machine.
   Let the loaf cool for 5 minutes.
   Gently shake the bucket to remove the loaf, and turn it out onto a rack to cool.

Beer and Cheese Bread

PREP: 10 MINUTES
Size: 1.5 pounds

Ingredients:
3 ½ cups bread or all-purpose four
1 tbsp instant yeast
1 tsp salt
1 tbsp sugar
1½ cup beer at room temperature
½ cup shredded monterey cheese
½ cup shredded edam cheese

Directions:
1. **Preparing the Ingredients.** Place all ingredients, except cheeses, in the bread pan in the liquid-dry-yeast layering.
   Put the pan in the Hamilton Beach bread machine.
2. **Select the Bake cycle.** Choose White bread. Press Start.
   When the kneading process is about to end, add the cheese.
   Wait until the loaf is cooked. The machine will automatically start the keep warm mode after the bread is complete. Let it stay in that mode for about 10 minutes before unplugging.
   Remove the pan and let it cool down for about 10 minutes.

Blue Cheese Onion Bread
PREP: 10 MINUTES
Size: 1.5 pounds

Ingredients:
1¼ cup water, at 80°F to 90°F
1 egg, at room temperature
1 tablespoon melted butter, cooled
¼ cup powdered skim milk
1 tablespoon sugar
¾ teaspoon salt
½ cup (2 ounces) crumbled blue cheese
1 tablespoon dried onion flakes
3 cups white bread flour
¼ cup instant mashed potato flakes
1 teaspoon bread machine or active dry yeast

Directions:
1. **Preparing the Ingredients.** Place the ingredients in your Hamilton Beach bread machine.
2. **Select the Bake cycle.** Program the machine for White bread, select light or medium crust, and press Start.
   When the loaf is done, remove the bucket from the machine.
   Let the loaf cool for 5 minutes.
   Gently shake the bucket to remove the loaf, and turn it out onto a rack to cool.

Cheese Loaf

PREP: 10 MINUTES
Size: 1.5 pounds

Ingredients:
2¼ cups flour
2 tsp instant yeast
1¾ cups water
4 tbsp sugar
1½ cup shredded cheddar cheese
2 tbsp parmesan cheese
1 tsp mustard
1 tsp paprika
2 tbsp minced white onion
⅓ cup butter

Directions:
1. **Preparing the Ingredients.** Place all ingredients in the bread pan in the liquid-dry-yeast layering.
   Put the pan in the Hamilton Beach bread machine.
2. **Select the Bake cycle.** Choose White bread and light crust.
   Press start and wait until the loaf is cooked. The machine will automatically start the keep warm mode after the bread is complete. Let it stay in that mode for about 10 minutes before unplugging.
   Remove the pan and let it cool down for about 10 minutes.

Double Cheese Bread

PREP: 10 MINUTES
Size: 1.5 pounds

Ingredients:
1¼ cups milk, at 80°F to 90°F
1 tablespoon butter, melted and cooled
2 tablespoons sugar
1 teaspoon salt
½ teaspoon freshly ground black pepper
Pinch cayenne pepper
1½ cups (6 ounces) shredded aged sharp Cheddar cheese
½ cup (2 ounces) shredded or grated Parmesan cheese
3 cups white bread flour
1¼ teaspoons bread machine or instant yeast

Directions:
1. **Preparing the Ingredients.** Place the ingredients in your Hamilton Beach bread machine.
2. **Select the Bake cycle.** Program the machine for White bread, select light or medium crust, and press Start.
   When the loaf is done, remove the bucket from the machine.
   Let the loaf cool for 5 minutes.
   Gently shake the bucket to remove the loaf, and turn it out onto a rack to cool.

Three Cheese Bread

PREP: 10 MINUTES
Size: 1.5 pounds

Ingredients:
3 cups bread or all-purpose flour
1¼ cup warm milk
2 tbsp oil
2 tbsp sugar
2¼ tsp instant yeast or 1 packet
1 cup cheddar cheese
½ cup parmesan cheese
½ cup mozzarella cheese

Directions:
1. **Preparing the Ingredients.** Place all ingredients in the bread pan in the liquid-dry-yeast layering.
   Put the pan in the Hamilton Beach bread machine.
2. **Select the Bake cycle.** Choose White bread.
   Press start and wait until the loaf is cooked. The machine will automatically start the keep warm mode after the bread is complete. Let it stay in that mode for about 10 minutes before unplugging.
   Remove the pan and let it cool down for about 10 minutes.

Spinach and Feta Whole Wheat Bread

PREP: 10 MINUTES
Size: 1.5 pounds

Ingredients:
3⅔ cups whole wheat flour
1½ tsp instant yeast
¼ cup unsalted butter, melted
1 cup lukewarm water
2 tbsp sugar
½ tsp salt
¾ cups blanched and chopped spinach, fresh
½ tsp pepper
½ tsp paprika
⅓ cup feta cheese, mashed

Directions:
1. **Preparing the Ingredients.** Place all ingredients, except spinach, butter, and feta, in the bread pan in the liquid-dry-yeast layering.
   Put the pan in the Hamilton Beach bread machine.
2. **Select the Bake cycle.** Choose Whole Wheat. Press start.
   When the dough has gathered, manually add the feta and spinach.
   Resume and wait until the loaf is cooked. Once cooked brush with butter.
   The machine will automatically start the keep warm mode after the bread is complete. Let it stay in that mode for about 10 minutes before unplugging.
   Remove the pan and let it cool down for about 10 minutes.

Mozzarella and Salami Bread

PREP: 10 MINUTES
Size: 1.5 pounds

Ingredients:
1 cup water plus 2 tablespoons, at 80°F to 90°F
½ cup (2 ounces) shredded mozzarella cheese
2 tablespoons sugar
1 teaspoon salt
1 teaspoon dried basil
¼ teaspoon garlic powder
3¼ cups white bread flour
1½ teaspoons bread machine or instant yeast
¾ cup finely diced hot German salami

Directions:
1. **Preparing the Ingredients.** Place the ingredients, except the salami, in your Hamilton Beach bread machine.
2. **Select the Bake cycle.** Program the machine for White bread, select light or medium crust, and press Start.
   Add the salami when your machine signals or 5 minutes before the second kneading cycle is finished.
   When the loaf is done, remove the bucket from the machine.
   Let the loaf cool for 5 minutes.
   Gently shake the bucket to remove the loaf, and turn it out onto a rack to cool.

Cheese Swirl Loaf

PREP: 15 MINUTES
Size: 1.5 pounds

Ingredients:
3 cups all purpose flour
1¼ cup lukewarm milk
3 tbsp sugar
1 tsp salt
1½ tsp instant yeast
3 tbsp melted butter
4 slices of monterey cheese
½ cup mozzarella cheese
½ cup edam or any quick melting cheese
½ tsp paprika

Directions:
1. **Preparing the Ingredients.** Place all ingredients, except cheeses, in the bread pan in the liquid-dry-yeast layering.
   Put the pan in the Hamilton Beach bread machine.
2. **Select the Bake cycle.** Choose White bread. Press start.
   Place all the cheese in a microwavable bowl. Melt in the microwave for 30 seconds. Cool, but make sure to keep soft.
   After 10 minutes into the kneading process, pause the machine. Take out half of the dough. Roll it flat on the work surface.
   Spread the cheese on the flat dough. Roll thinly. Return to the bread pan carefully.
   Resume and wait until the loaf is cooked. The machine will automatically start the keep warm mode after the bread is complete. Let it stay in that mode for about 10 minutes before unplugging.
   Remove the pan and let it cool down for about 10 minutes.

Chile Cheese Bacon Bread
PREP: 10 MINUTES
Size: 1.5 pounds

Ingredients:
½ cup milk, at 80°F to 90°F
1½ teaspoons melted butter, cooled
1½ tablespoons honey
1½ teaspoons salt
½ cup chopped and drained green chiles
½ cup (2 ounces) grated Cheddar cheese
½ cup chopped cooked bacon
3 cups white bread flour
2 teaspoons bread machine or instant yeast

Directions.
1. **Preparing the Ingredients.** Place the ingredients in your Hamilton Beach bread machine.
2. **Select the Bake cycle.** Program the machine for White bread, select light or medium crust, and press Start.
   When the loaf is done, remove the bucket from the machine.
   Let the loaf cool for 5 minutes.
   Gently shake the bucket to remove the loaf, and turn it out onto a rack to cool.

Italian Parmesan Bread

PREP: 10 MINUTES
Size: 1.5 pounds

Ingredients:
1 cup plus 2 tablespoons water, at 80°F to 90°F
3 tablespoons melted butter, cooled
1 tablespoon sugar
1 teaspoon salt
2 teaspoons chopped fresh basil
¼ cup grated Parmesan cheese
3½ cups white bread flour
1½ teaspoons bread machine or instant yeast

Directions:
1. **Preparing the Ingredients.** Place the ingredients in your Hamilton Beach bread machine.
2. **Select the Bake cycle.** Program the machine for White bread, select light or medium crust, and press Start.
   When the loaf is done, remove the bucket from the machine.
   Let the loaf cool for 5 minutes.
   Gently shake the bucket to remove the loaf, and turn it out onto a rack to cool.

Lava Cheese and Onion Bread

PREP: 10 MINUTES
Size: 1.5 pounds

Ingredients:
3 cups + 2 tbsp all-purpose flour
1 cup water
2 tbsp oil
2 tbsp sugar
3 tbsp milk
1 tbsp instant yeast
½ cup caramelized onion
1 cup mozzarella cheese
1 cup cheddar cheese

Directions:
1. **Preparing the Ingredients.** Place all ingredients, except onion and cheeses, in the bread pan in the liquid-dry-yeast layering.
   Put the pan in the Hamilton Beach bread machine.
2. **Select the Bake cycle.** Choose White bread. Press start.
   Before the baking process starts, pause the machine. Make a large incision at the center of the bun. Add the mozzarella cheese, top with caramelized onion, and sprinkle on the cheddar cheese.
   Resume and wait until the loaf is cooked. The machine will automatically start the keep warm mode after the bread is complete. Let it stay in that mode for about 10 minutes before unplugging.
   Remove the pan and let it cool down for about 10 minutes.

Feta Oregano Bread

PREP: 10 MINUTES
Size: 1.5 pounds

Ingredients:
1 cup milk, at 80°F to 90°F
1 tablespoon melted butter, cooled
1 tablespoon sugar
1 teaspoon salt
1 tablespoon dried oregano
3 cups white bread flour
2¼ teaspoons bread machine or instant yeast
1 cup (4 ounces) crumbled feta cheese

Directions:
1. **Preparing the Ingredients.** Place the ingredients in your Hamilton Beach bread machine.
2. **Select the Bake cycle.** Program the machine for White bread, select light or medium crust, and press Start.
   When the loaf is done, remove the bucket from the machine.
   Let the loaf cool for 5 minutes.
   Gently shake the bucket to remove the loaf, and turn it out onto a rack to cool.

Sweet Bread

Chocolate Chip Peanut Butter Banana Bread
PREP: 20 MINUTES
Size: 2 pounds

Ingredients:
2 bananas, mashed
2 eggs, at room temperature
½ cup melted butter, cooled
2 tablespoons milk, at room temperature
1 teaspoon pure vanilla extract
2 cups all-purpose flour
½ cup sugar
1¼ teaspoons baking powder
½ teaspoon baking soda
½ teaspoon salt
½ cup peanut butter chips
½ cup semisweet chocolate chips

Directions:
1. **Preparing the Ingredients.** Stir together the bananas, eggs, butter, milk, and vanilla in the Hamilton Beach bread machine bucket and set it aside.
   In a medium bowl, toss together the flour, sugar, baking powder, baking soda, salt, peanut butter chips, and chocolate chips.
   Add the dry ingredients to the bucket.
2. **Select the Bake cycle.** Program the machine for Quick bread, and press Start.
   When the loaf is done, stick a knife into it, and if it comes out clean, the loaf is done.
   If the loaf needs a few more minutes, check the control panel for a Bake Only button and extend the time by 10 minutes.
   When the loaf is done, remove the bucket from the machine.
   Let the loaf cool for 5 minutes.
   Gently shake the bucket to remove the loaf, and turn it out onto a rack to cool.

Portuguese Sweet Bread

PREP: 10 MINUTES
Size: 1.5 pounds

Ingredients:
3 cups + 2 tbsp all-purpose flour
1 cup water
2 tbsp oil
2 tbsp + ⅓ cup sugar
3 tbsp milk
1 tbsp + 2 tsp instant yeast
1 egg beaten

Directions:

1. **Preparing the Ingredients.** Place all ingredients in the bread pan in the liquid-dry-yeast layering.
   Put the pan in the Hamilton Beach bread machine.
2. **Select the Bake cycle.** Choose White bread.
   Press start and wait until the loaf is cooked. The machine will automatically start the keep warm mode after the bread is complete. Let it stay in that mode for about 10 minutes before unplugging.
   Remove the pan and let it cool down for about 10 minutes.

Sour Cream Maple Bread
PREP: 10 MINUTES
Size: 1.5 pounds

Ingredients:
½ cup plus 1 tablespoon water, at 80°F to 90°F
½ cup plus 1 tablespoon sour cream, at room temperature
2¼ tablespoons butter, at room temperature
1 tablespoon maple syrup
¾ teaspoon salt
2¾ cups white bread flour
1⅔ teaspoons bread machine or instant yeast

Directions:
1. **Preparing the Ingredients.** Place the ingredients in your Hamilton Beach bread machine.
2. **Select the Bake cycle.** Program the machine for White bread, select light or medium crust, and press Start.
   When the loaf is done, remove the bucket from the machine.
   Let the loaf cool for 5 minutes.
   Gently shake the bucket to remove the loaf, and turn it out onto a rack to cool.

Chocolate Amish Bread

PREP: 10 MINUTES
Size: 1.5 pounds

Ingredients:
2½ cups flour
⅔ cup unsweetened cocoa
⅔ cup sugar
2 tbsp oil
1 tbsp instant yeast
1 egg
1 cup boiling water
½ cup warm water

Directions:
1. **Preparing the Ingredients.** Pour the boiling water to the cocoa. Mix and set aside until lukewarm.
   Bloom the yeast by adding ½ cup water to the yeast.
   Place all ingredients in the Hamilton Beach bread pan in the liquid-dry-yeast layering.
   Put the pan in the Hamilton Beach bread machine.
2. **Select the Bake cycle.** Choose White bread
   Press start and wait until the loaf is cooked. The machine will automatically start the keep warm mode after the bread is complete. Let it stay in that mode for about 10 minutes before unplugging.
   Remove the pan and let it cool down for about 10 minutes.

Barmbrack Bread

PREP: 10 MINUTES
Size: 1.5 pounds

Ingredients:
1 cup plus 2 tablespoons water, at 80°F to 90°F
1½ tablespoons melted butter, cooled
3 tablespoons sugar
3 tablespoons skim milk powder
1½ teaspoons salt
1 teaspoon dried lemon zest
½ teaspoon ground allspice
¼ teaspoon ground nutmeg
3 cups white bread flour
2½ teaspoons bread machine or active dry yeast
¾ cup dried currants

Directions:
1. **Preparing the Ingredients.** Place the ingredients, except the currants, in your Hamilton Beach bread machine.
2. **Select the Bake cycle.** Program the Hamilton Beach for White bread, select light or medium crust, and press Start.
   Add the currants when your machine signals or when the second kneading cycle starts.
   When the loaf is done, remove the bucket from the machine.
   Let the loaf cool for 5 minutes.
   Gently shake the bucket to remove the loaf, and turn it out onto a rack to cool.

Gooey Cinnamon Roll

PREP: 10 MINUTES
Size: 1.5 pounds

Ingredients:
4 cups bread flour
1 cup warm milk
1 egg, beaten lightly
¼ cup sugar
¼ cup butter
2¼ tsp yeast or 1 packet
¼ cup warm water
¼ cup butter
½ cup packed brown sugar
1¼ tsp cinnamon powder

Directions:
1. **Preparing the Ingredients.** Place all ingredients, except butter, brown sugar, and cinnamon, in the Hamilton Beach bread pan in the liquid-dry-yeast layering.
Put the pan in the Hamilton Beach bread machine.
2. **Select the Bake cycle.** Choose Sweet breads medium.
Meanwhile, melt the butter. Add the brown sugar and cinnamon. Mix well.
Lightly flour the work surface. Take out the dough and cut into two equal portions. Roll each portion to about ½ inch thick.
Spread ½ of the cinnamon filling on top, but leave an edge unfilled. Roll into a log. Cut the dough to about 2 inch thick.
Do the same with the other portion.
Cover and proof for 30 minutes.
Bake in 360 degrees F in a preheated oven for 25 to 30 minutes.

Crusty Honey Bread

PREP: 10 MINUTES
Size: 1.5 pounds

Ingredients:
1 cup minus 1 tablespoon water, at 80°F to 90°F
1½ tablespoons honey
1⅛ tablespoons melted butter, cooled
¾ teaspoon salt
2⅔ cups white bread flour
1½ teaspoons bread machine or instant yeast

Directions:
1. **Preparing the Ingredients.** Place the ingredients in your Hamilton Beach bread machine.
2. **Select the Bake cycle.** Program the Hamilton Beach for White bread, select light or medium crust, and press Start.
   When the loaf is done, remove the bucket from the machine.
   Let the loaf cool for 5 minutes.
   Gently shake the bucket to remove the loaf, and turn it out onto a rack to cool.

Portuguese Sweet Bread

PREP: 10 MINUTES
Size: 1.5 pounds

Ingredients:
3 cups + 2 tbsp all-purpose flour
1 cup water
2 tbsp oil
2 tbsp + ⅓ cup sugar
3 tbsp milk
1 tbsp + 2 tsp instant yeast
1 egg beaten

Directions:
1. **Preparing the Ingredients.** Place all ingredients in the bread pan in the liquid-dry-yeast layering.
   Put the pan in the Hamilton Beach bread machine.
2. **Select the Bake cycle.** Choose Sweet Breads.
   Press start and wait until the loaf is cooked. The machine will automatically start the keep warm mode after the bread is complete. Let it stay in that mode for about 10 minutes before unplugging.
   Remove the pan and let it cool down for about 10 minutes.

Honey Granola Bread

PREP: 10 MINUTES
Size: 1.5 pounds

Ingredients:
1⅛ cups milk, at 80°F to 90°F
3 tablespoons honey
1½ tablespoons butter, melted and cooled
1⅛ teaspoons salt
¾ cup whole-wheat flour
⅔ cup prepared granola, crushed
1¾ cups white bread flour
1½ teaspoons bread machine or instant yeast

Directions:
1. **Preparing the Ingredients.** Place the ingredients in your Hamilton Beach bread machine.
2. **Select the Bake cycle.** Program the Hamilton Beach for Sweet breads, select light or medium crust, and press Start.
   When the loaf is done, remove the bucket from the machine.
   Let the loaf cool for 5 minutes.
   Gently shake the bucket to remove the loaf, and turn it out onto a rack to cool.

Custard Filled Dinner Rolls

PREP: 10 MINUTES
Size: 1.5 pounds

Ingredients:
    For the bread:
1 cups warm milk
4 cups bread flour
4 tbsp sugar
2 tsp instant dry yeast
2 eggs
¾ cup butter
egg wash
    For the custard:
⅓ cup sugar
1 cup milk
1½ tbsp bread flour
3 egg yolks
1 tbsp butter

Directions:
1. **Preparing the Ingredients.** Make the dough. Place the yeast, 4 tbsp sugar, and 1 cup milk in the pan. Bloom the yeast for at least 5 minutes.
   Add the 2 eggs and the 4 cups flour.
2. **Select the Bake cycle.** Choose Sweet Breads. Press Start.
   After five minutes, add ¾ cup butter and wait for the cycle to finish.
   Make the custard. Start by scalding the remaining milk and butter in a saucepan. Set aside. In another bowl, whisk the egg yolks. Add the remaining flour and sugar until incorporated. Whisk in half of the milk mixture. Return to the saucepan. Mix.
   Heat mix on low heat until sticky. Cover with plastic wrap and set aside to cool.
   Remove the dough.
   Cut into equal slices and roll each slice flat. Place a tbsp of the custard. Gather the edges and seal.
   Arrange in the baking sheet. Proof for 30 seconds.
   Brush with egg wash. Bake for 25 minutes in a preheated oven at 360 degrees F.

Vanilla Almond Milk Bread

PREP: 10 MINUTES
Size: 1.5 pounds

Ingredients:
½ cup plus 1 tablespoon milk, at 80°F to 90°F
3 tablespoons melted butter, cooled
3 tablespoons sugar
1 egg, at room temperature
1½ teaspoons pure vanilla extract
⅓ teaspoon almond extract
2½ cups white bread flour
1½ teaspoons bread machine or instant yeast

Directions:
1. **Preparing the Ingredients.** Place the ingredients in your Hamilton Beach bread machine.
2. **Select the Bake cycle.** Program the machine for Sweet breads, select light or medium crust, and press Start.
   When the loaf is done, remove the bucket from the machine.
   Let the loaf cool for 5 minutes.
   Gently shake the bucket to remove the loaf, and turn it out onto a rack to cool.

Chocolate Oatmeal Banana Bread
PREP: 10 MINUTES
Size: 1.5 pounds

Ingredients:
3 bananas, mashed
2 eggs, at room temperature
¾ cup packed light brown sugar
½ cup (1 stick) butter, at room temperature
½ cup sour cream, at room temperature
¼ cup sugar
1½ teaspoons pure vanilla extract
1 cup all-purpose flour
½ cup quick oats
2 tablespoons unsweetened cocoa powder
1 teaspoon baking soda

Directions:
1. **Preparing the Ingredients.** Place the banana, eggs, brown sugar, butter, sour cream, sugar, and vanilla in your Hamilton Beach bread machine.
2. **Select the Bake cycle.** Program the machine for Sweet breads and press Start.
    While the wet ingredients are mixing, stir together the flour, oats, cocoa powder, and baking soda in a small bowl.
    After the first fast mixing is done and the machine signals, add the dry ingredients.
    When the loaf is done, remove the bucket from the machine.
    Let the loaf cool for 5 minutes.
    Gently shake the bucket to remove the loaf, and turn it out onto a rack to cool.

Pumpkin Coconut Bread
PREP: 10 MINUTES
Size: 1.5 pounds

Ingredients:
1 cup pure canned pumpkin
½ cup (1 stick) butter, at room temperature
1½ teaspoons pure vanilla extract
1 cup sugar
½ cup dark brown sugar
2 cups all-purpose flour
¾ cup sweetened shredded coconut
1½ teaspoons ground cinnamon
1 teaspoon baking soda
1 teaspoon baking powder
½ teaspoon ground nutmeg
½ teaspoon ground ginger
⅛ teaspoon ground allspice

Directions:
1. **Preparing the Ingredients.** Place the pumpkin, butter, vanilla, sugar, and dark brown sugar in your Hamilton Beach bread machine.
2. **Select the Bake cycle.** Program the machine for Rapid Sweet breads and press Start. After the first fast mixing is done, add the flour, coconut, cinnamon, baking soda, baking powder, nutmeg, ginger, and allspice.
   When the loaf is done, remove the bucket from the machine.
   Let the loaf cool for 5 minutes.
   Gently shake the bucket to remove the loaf, and turn it out onto a rack to cool.

Chocolate Chip Bread

PREP: 10 MINUTES
Size: 1.5 pounds

Ingredients:
3 cups flour
1 cup milk
⅓ cup sugar
2 tbsp oil
1 tbsp instant yeast
1 egg
1 tbsp cinnamon
¼ cup brown sugar
1 cup semi-sweet chocolate chips

Directions:

1. **Preparing the Ingredients.** Bloom the yeast with milk and 2 tbsp of sugar for at least 5 minutes in the pan.
   Place all ingredients, except chocolate chips, in the Hamilton Beach bread pan in the liquid-dry-yeast layering.
   Put the pan in the Hamilton Beach bread machine.
   Load the chocolate chips in the automatic dispenser.
2. **Select the Bake cycle.** Choose Rapid Sweet breads.
   Press start and wait until the loaf is cooked. The machine will automatically start the keep warm mode after the bread is complete. Let it stay in that mode for about 10 minutes before unplugging.
   Remove the pan and let it cool down for about 10 minutes.

Gluten-Free Bread

Gluten-Free White Bread
PREP: 10 MINUTES
Size: 1.5 pounds

Ingredients:
- 2 cups white rice flour
- 1 cup potato starch
- ½ cup soy flour
- ½ cup cornstarch
- 1 tsp vinegar
- 1 tsp xanthan gum
- 1 tsp instant yeast (bread yeast should be gluten free, but always check)
- 1¼ cup buttermilk
- 3 eggs
- ¼ cup sugar or honey
- ¼ cup coconut or olive oil

Directions:
1. **Preparing the Ingredients.** Place all ingredients in the Hamilton Beach bread pan in the liquid-dry-yeast layering.
   Put the pan in the Hamilton Beach bread machine.
2. **Select the Bake cycle.** Choose WhiteBread. Press Start.
   Five minutes into the kneading process, pause the machine and check the consistency of the dough. Add more flour if necessary.
   Resume and wait until the loaf is cooked. The machine will automatically start the keep warm mode after the bread is complete. Let it stay in that mode for about 10 minutes before unplugging.
   Remove the pan and let it cool down for about 10 minutes.

Brown Rice Bread

PREP: 10 MINUTES
Size: 1.5 pounds

Ingredients:
- brown rice flour
- 2 eggs
- 1¼ cup almond milk
- 1 tsp vinegar
- ½ cup coconut oil
- 2 tbsp sugar
- ½ tsp salt
- 2¼ tsp instant yeast (bread yeast should be gluten free, but always check)

Directions:
1. **Preparing the Ingredients.** Place all ingredients in the Hamilton Beach bread pan in the liquid-dry-yeast layering.
   Put the pan in the Hamilton Beach bread machine.
2. **Select the Bake cycle.** Choose White Bread. Press Start.
   Five minutes into the kneading process, pause the machine and check the consistency of the dough. Add more flour if necessary.
   Resume and wait until the loaf is cooked. The machine will automatically start the keep warm mode after the bread is complete. Let it stay in that mode for about 10 minutes before unplugging.
   Remove the pan and let it cool down for about 10 minutes.

Brown Rice and Cranberry Bread

PREP: 10 MINUTES
Size: 1.5 pounds

Ingredients:
- 3 eggs, beaten
- 1 tsp white vinegar
- 3 tbsp gluten-free oil
- 1½ cup lukewarm water
- 3 cups brown rice flour
- 1 tbsp xanthan gum
- ¼ cup flaxseed meal
- 1 tsp salt
- ¼ cup sugar
- ½ cup powdered milk
- ⅔ cup cranberries, dried and cut into bits
- 2¼ tsp instant yeast (bread yeast should be gluten free, but always check)

Directions:
1. **Preparing the Ingredients.** Mix all the wet and the dry ingredients, except the yeast and cranberries, separately.
   Place all ingredients in the Hamilton Beach bread pan in the liquid-dry-yeast layering. Put the pan in the Hamilton Beach bread machine.
   Load the cranberries in the automatic dispenser.
2. **Select the Bake cycle.** Choose White Bread. Press start and wait until the loaf is cooked. The machine will automatically start the keep warm mode after the bread is complete. Let it stay in that mode for about 10 minutes before unplugging.
   Remove the pan and let it cool down for about 10 minutes. Layer them in the bread machine, in the liquid-dry-yeast layering. Do not add the cranberries.

Gluten-Free Peasant Bread

PREP: 10 MINUTES
Size: 1.5 pounds

Ingredients:
- 2 cups brown rice flour
- 1 cup potato starch
- 1 tbsp xanthan gum
- 2 tbsp sugar
- 2 tbsp yeast (bread yeast should be gluten free, but always check)
- 3 tbsp vegetable oil
- 5 eggs
- 1 tsp white vinegar

Directions:
1. **Preparing the Ingredients.** Bloom the yeast in water with the sugar for five minutes. Place all ingredients in the Hamilton Beach bread pan in the yeast-liquid-dry layering. Put the pan in the Hamilton Beach bread machine.
2. **Select the Bake cycle.** Choose White Bread. Press start and wait until the loaf is cooked. The machine will automatically start the keep warm mode after the bread is complete. Let it stay in that mode for about 10 minutes before unplugging. Remove the pan and let it cool down for about 10 minutes.

Gluten-Free Hawaiian Loaf

PREP: 10 MINUTES
Size: 1.5 pounds

Ingredients:
- 4 cups gluten-free four
- 1 tsp xanthan gum
- 2½ tsp (bread yeast should be gluten free, but always check)
- ¼ cup white sugar
- ½ cup softened butter
- 1 egg, beaten
- 1 cup fresh pineapple juice, warm
- ½ tsp salt
- 1 tsp vanilla extract

Directions:

1. **Preparing the Ingredients.** Place all ingredients in the Hamilton Beach bread pan in the liquid-dry-yeast layering.
   Put the pan in the Hamilton Beach bread machine.
2. **Select the Bake cycle.** Choose White Bread. Press start and wait until the loaf is cooked. The machine will automatically start the keep warm mode after the bread is complete. Let it stay in that mode for about 10 minutes before unplugging.
   Remove the pan and let it cool down for about 10 minutes.

Vegan Gluten-Free Bread

PREP: 10 MINUTES
Size: 1.5 pounds

Ingredients:
- 1 cup almond flour
- 1 cup brown or white rice flour
- 2 tbsp potato flour
- 4 tsp baking powder
- ¼ tsp baking soda
- 1 cup almond milk
- 1 tbsp white vinegar

Directions:
1. **Preparing the Ingredients.** Place all ingredients in the Hamilton Beach bread pan in the liquid-dry-yeast layering.
   Put the pan in the Hamilton Beach bread machine.
2. **Select the Bake cycle.** Choose White Bread. Press start and wait until the loaf is cooked. The machine will automatically start the keep warm mode after the bread is complete. Let it stay in that mode for about 10 minutes before unplugging. Remove the pan and let it cool down for about 10 minutes.

Sourdough Breads

Sourdough Starter
PREP: 10 MINUTES
Size: 1.5 pounds

Ingredients:
- 2 tsp instant yeast
- 1¼ + ½ cup lukewarm water
- 2¼ + 1 cups bread flour

Directions:
1. **Preparing the Ingredients.** Stir the yeast into 1¼ cups lukewarm water in a large glass or stainless bowl. Gradually add 2¼ cups flour and mix until lump free. Cover with clean cloth or cling wrap. Set aside for 5 days in a dry place to bloom. After five days, the yeast in this mixture is still vigorous. You need to weaken it.
2. Measure the mixture. Discard half of it.
3. Stir in another ½ cup of water and 1 cup of flour into the remaining first mixture. Mix until combined.
4. This is the "feeding" stage. You need to feed the yeast to make it bloom. However, since the yeast has been reduced, it becomes weaker.
5. Cover the mixture with cling wrap or clean cloth. Let it stand at room temperature for another 2 days. It takes at least 2 days for the yeast to bloom again because it is weaker.
6. After two days, your starter is ready.

Oat Sourdough Loaf

PREP: 10 MINUTES
Size: 1.5 pounds

Ingredients:
- 3 cups whole wheat or bread flour
- 250g starter (see Sourdough Starter recipe)
- ½ cup water
- 3 tbsp honey
- 1 tbsp dark brown sugar or honey
- 1 stick butter, melted
- 1 tbsp instant yeast
- 1 tsp salt
- ¾ quick cooking oatmeal

Directions:
1. **Preparing the Ingredients.** Grind the oatmeal in the food processor and combine with the rest of the dry ingredients, except yeast, in a bowl.
   Place all the liquid ingredients in bread pan. Add the starter, dry mix then the yeast.
   Put the pan in the Hamilton Beach bread machine.
2. **Select the Bake cycle.** Choose White Bread. Press start and wait until the loaf is cooked. The machine will automatically start the keep warm mode after the bread is complete. Let it stay in that mode for about 10 minutes before unplugging.
   Remove the pan and let it cool down for about 10 minutes.

Whole-Wheat Sourdough Bread
PREP: 10 MINUTES
Size: 1.5 pounds

Ingredients:
- ¾ cup plus 2 tablespoons water, at 80°F to 90°F
- ¾ cup plus 2 tablespoons No-Yeast Whole-Wheat Sourdough Starter, fed, active, and at room temperature (See Sourdough Starter recipe)

- 2 tablespoons melted butter, cooled
- 1 tablespoon sugar
- 1½ teaspoons salt
- 3 cups whole-wheat flour
- 1¾ teaspoons bread machine or instant yeast

Directions:
1. **Preparing the Ingredients.** Place the ingredients in your Hamilton Beach bread machine.
2. **Select the Bake cycle.** Program the Hamilton Beach for Whole-Grain bread, select light or medium crust, and press Start. When the loaf is done, remove the bucket from the machine. Let the loaf cool for 5 minutes.

   Gently shake the bucket to remove the loaf, and turn it out onto a rack to cool.

Basic Sourdough Loaf

PREP: 10 MINUTES
Size: 1.5 pounds

Ingredients:
- 3 cups bread flour
- 225g starter (see Sourdough Starter recipe)
- ½ cup warm water
- 1 tsp salt
- 1½ tsp sugar
- 1 tbsp oil

Directions:
1. **Preparing the Ingredients.** Add the water and the starter to the bread pan. Add the oil, sugar, flour and the salt.
   Place all ingredients in the bread pan in the liquid-dry-yeast layering.
   Put the pan in the Hamilton Beach bread machine.
2. **Select the Bake cycle.** Choose White Bread. Press start and wait until the loaf is cooked.
   The machine will automatically start the keep warm mode after the bread is complete. Let it stay in that mode for about 10 minutes before unplugging.
   Remove the pan and let it cool down for about 10 minutes.

Multigrain Sourdough Bread

PREP: 10 MINUTES
Size: 1.5 pounds

Ingredients:
- ⅔ cup water, at 80°F to 90°F
- ¾ cup Simple Sourdough Starter (See Sourdough Starter recipe), fed, active, and at room temperature
- 2 tablespoons melted butter, cooled
- 2½ tablespoons sugar
- ¾ teaspoon salt
- ¾ cup multigrain cereal (Bob's Red Mill or equivalent)
- 2⅔ cups white bread flour
- 1½ teaspoons bread machine or instant yeast

Directions:
1. **Preparing the Ingredients.** Place the ingredients in your Hamilton Beach bread machine.
2. **Select the Bake cycle.** Program the machine for Whole-Grain bread, select light or medium crust, and press Start.
   When the loaf is done, remove the bucket from the machine.
   Let the loaf cool for 5 minutes.
   Gently shake the bucket to remove the loaf, and turn it out onto a rack to cool.

Sourdough Milk Bread

PREP: 10 MINUTES
Size: 1.5 pounds

Ingredients:
- 1½ cups Simple Sourdough Starter (See Sourdough Starter recipe), fed, active, and at room temperature
- ⅓ cup milk, at 80°F to 90°F
- 3 tablespoons olive oil
- 1½ tablespoons honey
- 1 teaspoon salt
- 3 cups white bread flour
- 1 teaspoon bread machine or instant yeast

Directions:
1. **Preparing the Ingredients.** Place the ingredients in your Hamilton Beach bread machine.
2. **Select the Bake cycle.** Program the machine for White bread, select light or medium crust, and press Start.
   When the loaf is done, remove the bucket from the machine.
   Let the loaf cool for 5 minutes.
   Gently shake the bucket to remove the loaf, and turn it out onto a rack to cool.

Sourdough Beer Bread

PREP: 10 MINUTES
Size: 1.5 pounds

Ingredients:
- 1 cup Simple Sourdough Starter (See Sourdough Starter recipe) fed, active, and at room temperature
- ½ cup plus 1 tablespoon dark beer, at 80°F to 90°F
- 1½ tablespoons melted butter, cooled
- ¾ tablespoon sugar
- 1⅛ teaspoons salt
- 2⅔ cups white bread flour
- 1⅛ teaspoons bread machine or instant yeast

Directions:
1. **Preparing the Ingredients.** Place the ingredients in your Hamilton Beach bread machine.
2. **Select the Bake cycle.** Program the machine for French Bread, select light or medium crust, and press Start.
   When the loaf is done, remove the bucket from the machine.
   Let the loaf cool for 5 minutes.
   Gently shake the bucket to remove the loaf, and turn it out onto a rack to cool.

Crusty Sourdough Bread

PR PREP: 10 MINUTES
Size: 1.5 pounds

Ingredients:
- 1 cup Simple Sourdough Starter (See Sourdough Starter recipe), fed, active, and at room temperature
- ½ cup water, at 80°F to 90°F
- 2 tablespoons honey
- 1½ teaspoons salt
- 3 cups white bread flour
- 1 teaspoon bread machine or instant yeast

Directions:
1. **Preparing the Ingredients.** Place the ingredients in your Hamilton Beach bread machine.
2. **Select the Bake cycle.** Program the machine for White bread, select light or medium crust, and press Start.
   When the loaf is done, remove the bucket from the machine.
   Let the loaf cool for 5 minutes.
   Gently shake the bucket to remove the loaf, and turn it out onto a rack to cool.

Herb Sourdough
PREP: 10 MINUTES
Size: 1.5 pounds

Ingredients:
- 2 cups No-Yeast Sourdough Starter (See Sourdough Starter recipe), fed, active, and at room temperature
- 2 tablespoons water, at 80°F to 90°F
- 2 tablespoons melted butter, cooled
- 2 teaspoons sugar
- 1½ teaspoons salt
- 1½ teaspoons chopped fresh basil
- 1½ teaspoons chopped fresh oregano
- 1 teaspoon chopped fresh thyme
- 2½ cups white bread flour
- 1½ teaspoons bread machine or instant yeast

Directions:
1. **Preparing the Ingredients.** Place the ingredients in your Hamilton Beach bread machine.
2. **Select the Bake cycle.** Program the machine for White bread, select light or medium crust, and press Start.
   When the loaf is done, remove the bucket from the machine.
   Let the loaf cool for 5 minutes.
   Gently shake the bucket to remove the loaf, and turn it out onto a rack to cool.

ERITAGE OF FOOD: A FAMILY GATHERING

To survive, we need to eat. As a result, food has turned into a symbol of loving, nurturing and sharing with one another. Recording, collecting, sharing and remembering the recipes that have been passed to you by your family is a great way to immortalize and honor your family. It is these traditions that carve out your individual personality. You will not just be honoring your family tradition by cooking these recipes, but they will also inspire you to create your own variations, which you can then pass on to your children's.

The recipes are just passed on to everyone, and nobody actually possesses them. I too love sharing recipes. The collection is vibrant and rich as a number of home cooks have offered their inputs to ensure that all of us can cook delicious meals at our home. I am thankful to each one of you who has contributed to this book and has allowed their traditions to pass on and grow with others. You guys are wonderful!

I am also thankful to the cooks who have evaluated all these recipes. You're, as well as, the comments that came from your family members and friends were invaluable.

If you have the time and inclination, please consider leaving a short review wherever you can, we would love to learn more about your opinion.

https://www.amazon.com/review/review-your-purchases/

About the Author

Amanda is a New York-based food writer, experienced chef. She loves sharing Easy, Delicious and Healthy recipes, especially the delicious and healthy meals that can be prepared using her Bread Machine. Amanda is a passionate advocate for the health benefits of a low-carb lifestyle. When she's not cooking, Amanda enjoys spending time with her husband and her kids, gardening and traveling.

CPSIA information can be obtained
at www.ICGtesting.com
Printed in the USA
BVHW010350080221
599613BV00017B/524